TO MY BESTIE,

_____

FROM YOUR BESTIE,

_____

ABBY PHIL TOM HEIDI SHIRLEY LEO LEEANN LOIS RICHARD SUSIE

ADAM DANA JAN DAVID JANET ALI PETER ELI TIM SUSAN MELISSA

CARA JULIA CHRIS STEPHANIE PAISLEY NAOMI PAUL MARNIE JOANNE

MEG GARY JOE MJ JOYCE AMY MICHELLE MEL JENNA TERRY SONA

LY BARB MARY BOB ARON JEREMY SANFORD MARILYN KAYLA MURPHY

JAMES STEPHEN PEGGY MIKE SUE CINDY JULIE LISA JONATHAN TIM

DIANE DAVID JIMMY STELLA CAROLYN ANDREW EMILY BARBARA FRED

MEGAN MARK EDDIE CHERYL PILAR JIMMY KEN AUNT ESTHER RACHEL

E ELLEN STEVE CHERYL TAHRA GARY SHARLEEN TONY DAVID MIERTA

JOHN HARRISON MADELINE JEREMY ABBY PHIL TOM HEIDI SHIRLEY

BIN BILL TRACY ERIKA ALESSANDRA ADAM DANA JAN DAVID JANET

MICHAEL HARRIET JONAH EMMA RON CARA JULIA CHRIS STEPHANIE

TOM PENELOPE DEEPAK FARLEY MICHAEL MEG GARY JOE MJ JOYCE

SA BILL CARRIE CONNIE PAM NICOLE SALLY BARB MARY BOB ARON

WYATT AL MAUREEN JENNY JOE KATE LILY JAMES STEPHEN PEGGY

INDSAY MEL RICHIE JON WENDY PATTI SCOTT DIANE DAVID JIMMY

SANNE RALPH CHANEL CHERYL MICHAEL KATIE SEAN MEGAN MARK

ANEANE LIZA ZOE JIM KATHRYN SALLY JIM DEB ANNIE ELLEN STEVE

ANTHA SHELLEY POLLY STUART CIEL LEO JENNIFER JOHN HARRISON

RICHARD SUSIE JENNIFER JON JEMMA BECKETT ROBIN BILL TRACY

SUSAN MELISSA MARY (SISTER SLEDGE) JULIE JILL MICHAEL HARRIET

ARNIE JOANNE BOB ANN KRISTEN GAIL KATHY TOM PENELOPE DEEPAK

TERRY SONA KATIE KERITH HILLARY THERESA BILL CARRIE CONNIE

N KAYLA MURPHY PETE DEIRDRE JOE SEANA WYATT AL MAUREEN

E LISA JONATHAN TIM LUCY SCOTT THERESE LINDSAY MEL RICHIE

V EMILY BARBARA FRED MILLIE AUNT RUTH SUSANNE RALPH CHANEL

MY KEN AUNT ESTHER RACHEL FREIDA MARLO JEANEANE LIZA ZOE

Y SHARLEEN TONY DAVID MIERTA NICKI CAREN SAMANTHA SHELLEY

BILLIONS *of* BESTIES

A CELEBRATION *of* FASCINATING *and* SIMPLY EXCEPTIONAL FRIENDSHIPS

PEGGY PANOSH x SUSIE ARONS
Illustrated by Peggy Panosh

TILLER PRESS

NEW YORK   LONDON   TORONTO   SYDNEY   NEW DELHI

TILLER PRESS

An Imprint of Simon & Schuster, Inc.
1230 Avenue of the Americas
New York, NY 10020

First Tiller Press hardcover edition October 2020

This publication contains the opinions and ideas of its author. It is intended to provide helpful and informative material on the subjects addressed in the publication. It is sold with the understanding that the author and publisher are not engaged in rendering medical, health, or any other kind of personal, professional services in the book. The reader should consult his or her medical, health, or other competent professional before adopting any of the suggestions in this book or drawing inferences from it.

The author and publisher specifically disclaim all responsibility for any liability, loss, or risk, personal or otherwise, that is incurred as a consequence, directly or indirectly, of the use and application of any of the contents of this book.

TILLER PRESS and colophon are trademarks of Simon & Schuster, Inc.

For information about special discounts for bulk purchases, please contact Simon & Schuster Special Sales at 1-866-506-1949 or business@simonandschuster.com.

The Simon & Schuster Speakers Bureau can bring authors to your live event. For more information or to book an event, contact the Simon & Schuster Speakers Bureau at 1-866-248-3049 or visit our website at www.simonspeakers.com.

Interior design by Matt Ryan

Manufactured in the United States of America

1   3   5   7   9   10   8   6   4   2

Library of Congress Cataloging-in-Publication Data

Names: Panosh, Peggy, author, illustrator. | Arons, Susie, author.
Title: Billions of besties : a celebration of fascinating and simply exceptional friendships / Peggy Panosh + Susie Arons ; illustrated by Peggy Panosh.
Other titles: Celebration of fascinating and simply exceptional friendships
Description: First Tiller Press hardcover edition. | New York, NY : Tiller Press, An Imprint of Simon & Schuster, Inc., 2020.
Identifiers: LCCN 2020021259 (print) | LCCN 2020021260 (ebook) | ISBN 9781982149857 (hardcover) | ISBN 9781982149871 (ebook)
Subjects: LCSH: Best friends—Anecdotes. | Celebrities—Anecdotes. | Friendship—Anecdotes. | Characters and characteristics.
Classification: LCC BF575.F66 P35 2020 (print) | LCC BF575.F66 (ebook) | DDC 177/.62--dc23
LC record available at https://lccn.loc.gov/2020021259
LC ebook record available at https://lccn.loc.gov/2020021260

ISBN 978-1-9821-4985-7
ISBN 978-1-9821-4987-1 (ebook)

FROM PEGGY PANOSH
For my family—Polly, Stuart, Ciel, Leo, Jennifer,
John, Madeline, Harrison, Tom, Heidi,
Phil + Abby—the most loving, lively + supportive
goofballs I could ever ask for.

FROM SUSIE ARONS
Every day I carry this pitch-perfect
trio in my heart. Bob, Aron + Jeremy,
you make everything matter.
Best. Most. Always.

CONTENTS

BILLIONS OF BESTIES IS A CELEBRATION OF BEST FRIENDS.

BESTIES ARE SOULMATES. They get each other. There are all kinds of besties and we can even have more than one. Friendships evolve over time—sometimes they grow together, other times they drift apart and come back together again. Whether we call them our BFF, bae, pal, babe, best mate, muffin, buddy, boo, bro, doll, soul sister, or superfriend, besties have a bond that cannot always be described but is always magical.

Our quest was to create a book that shines a light on some of the most engaging, funny, inspirational, and sometimes unexpected best friends that existed in real life as well as those that have been created throughout generations of art, culture, and entertainment. Whether in books, movies, television, theater, art, music, fashion, or cartoons, from the beginning of time, billions of best friends have come together to forge relationships that cannot always be explained, except by the besties themselves. And when you have someone's back, that is all the explanation that is needed.

We curated and explored all of the friendships in this book for you through our lens of curiosity, respect, and positivity and sprinkled it with an abundance of delight and a little bit of a wink. We hope you share it with *your* besties and have as much fun reading it as we did making it!

In the spirit of friendship + love,

Peggy + Susie

P.S. Thank you, Bob, for not opening the pool on time ;)

Chapter 1
CLASSICS

OG. Gold standard. Legendary. When you ask people to define best friends, there is one friendship that is always celebrated and often emulated:

OPRAH + GAYLE

THEY HAVE CAPTURED the ideals we all look for in a best friend: pure love, boundless joy, and unwavering support. They lift each other up, revel in each other's highs, comfort each other during the lows, always finding time for laughter and delight. Gayle is the mother, sister, touchstone that Oprah always wanted. Oprah is the advocate, the sounding board, and soul sister for Gayle. For more than 40 years, they have spoken nearly every single day. They revel in their individual successes and bask in each other's bright light. Their friendship is the North Star of friendships. It is transcendent. It is enduring. It is truly inspiring.

AMY POEHLER
+
TINA FEY

AMY: What sums up our friendship best? Mmmhh . . . how about that people believed it when I said we were actually like the Olsen twins and came from the same womb, which is why my pinkie and your thumb had the same fingerprint?

TINA: No. I think it was that we first bonded when we were like 22 or 23, at the ImprovOlympic Theater, and I taught you that you could either pluck your eyebrows or have a lady put hot wax on them. It was your first real beauty lesson.

AMY: How about that time when you had two girls and I had two boys and we already planned their weddings to each other and what we were going to wear (peach, which you also checked was going to be on trend in 20 years).

TINA: Or the time we were the first lady "Weekend Update" anchors on *SNL* or the only women Golden Globe hosts in 2013, 2014, and, oh yeah, in 2015. And then opened the 2019 Oscars with Maya.

AMY: I liked it when you said in an interview that we have tremendous respect for each other and when we first started working together it was like two beautiful baby lions who were put in a cage and didn't eat each other. That was beautiful.

TINA: And true.

(P.S. You know those conversations you dream/pretend happen if you were actually friends with celebrities you imagine/pretend you are friends with? You don't do that? Never mind! Facts true, conversation never happened.)

BERT + ERNIE

SOMETIMES THE REAL WORLD is so scary and stressful that good news—and we mean really sweet, practically unreal good news—is hard to believe. Like the 50-plus-year forever friendship of Bert and Ernie, the seven-year-olds who share their very own apartment on Sesame Street. Sure, you're probably saying there is no way a guy as serious and analytical as Bert, who loves oatmeal and playing checkers, would *EVER* hang out with a goofball like Ernie. I mean Ernie's favorite thing, besides playing jokes on Bert and playing washtub musical instruments with that guy Jimmy Fallon, is singing in the bathtub with his Rubber Duckie! But it's true. Just ask Bert's pet pigeon, Bernice!

CARL REINER + MEL BROOKS

8 p.m., La-Z-Boys in position? CHECK. ✓

TV trays? CHECK. ✓

What's for dinner? Whaddya think? Chicken? Roast Beef?
I don't know, maybe chicken, maybe roast beef. CHECK. CHECK. ✓✓

JEOPARDY!? JEOPARDY! CHECK. CHECK. CHECK. ✓✓✓

Unless you want a movie. You want a movie? Mmmhh, tell me about
it. Well, it's got the following lines: "Lock all the doors," "Secure the
perimeter," "Let nobody in and out," and "Get some rest." Sounds perfect.
For more than 60 years, until Reiner's death at age 98 in July 2020, these
two menschiest of mensches were by each other's side. And as Carl Reiner
proudly told Judy Woodruff, his life is fuller because of it. Ours too.

SAMUEL L. JACKSON + SPIKE LEE

MOREHOUSE MEN. Friends. Artistic collaborators and occasional artistic pugilists for more than 40 years—unconventional, but what else would you expect from this particular pair? Yet when Spike Lee finally won his long overdue Oscar in 2019 for *BlacKkKlansman* it was only fitting that Samuel L. Jackson was onstage to catch the hug that launched thousands of memes, tweets, and love notes from around the world—each one of them celebrating this outsized friendship. As *USA Today* TV critic Kelly Lawler tweeted later that day, "If I live my whole life and get a friend who loves me as much as Samuel L. Jackson loves Spike Lee I will have lived a damn good life."

MARTIN SCORSESE + ROBERT DE NIRO

"YOU TALKIN' TO ME?" is the iconic dialogue best identified with the 90-mph-talking director's film *Taxi Driver* and delivered by his famously understated BFF actor pal, known more for a wry smile or cocked eyebrow than any kind of small talk. While we recognize these good fellas as symbolic brothers of New York City and larger-than-life lions of their profession, having made 10 films together, we affectionately embrace Marty and Bob as best friends and passionate artists. They met on the mean streets of New York more than 60 years ago, but it was the crime drama *Mean Streets* that brought them together way back when. It's no surprise that art-imitating-life dialogue sprang up throughout their partnership; "Never rat on your friends and always keep your mouth shut." They are old-school rebels who share an unwavering loyalty, trust, extraordinary friendship, and the occasional bottle of bold red wine and plate of al dente pasta.

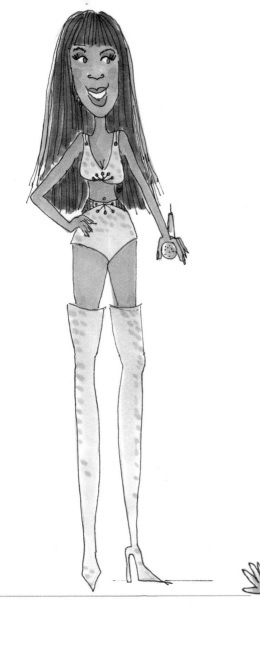

BEYONCÉ
+
KELLY ROWLAND

SISTERS-BESTIES.
That's what happens when
you meet as nine-year-olds,
singing your hearts out to
Whitney Houston onstage,
not knowing that destiny
was about to take you
future superstars on an
epic journey.

WITH MILLIONS OF RECORDS, movie star moments, and a few crashes, but no real burns between them, Bey and Kelly share a forever bond stronger than steel. Both of them know and praise the sisterhood circle that has surrounded them with the love and strength of a mother like no other in Tina Knowles-Lawson, sister Solange, and BFF Michelle Williams. They are SURVIVORS! As Beyoncé once shared for millions of friends in a birthday Insta, the love between these two is Big and runs deeeep. Amen.

STEVEN SPIELBERG + TOM HANKS

THEY WERE FRIENDS before they worked together, just two
neighborhood dads talking shop, kids running in and about, when
after about 10 years, in 1998, they found their first project. Lesser
beings might toe-dip when working with a friend for the first time.
But these two chose to go full-on, headfirst into the epic war drama
Saving Private Ryan. If they were worried for even a split second that
their friendship might not survive the trials of the shoot, five films
later the rest is, as they say—and in this case, very literally—history.
Hanks has been called not just the nicest man in showbiz, but maybe
the nicest man EVER. For Spielberg, pick a superlative: legendary,
genius, giant, Picasso . . . Both men stand up proudly for social
justice and freedom, through their films and work off camera. While
promoting 2017's *The Post*, Cinemablend said, "Steven Spielberg and
Tom Hanks is a combination that has gone down in history as one of
those peanut butter/chocolate mashups that usually brings something
beautiful to the table." The same can be seen in and said
of this enduring friendship, a public admiration as comfortable
as a well-worn tweed jacket or cable-knit cardigan.

JON STEWART +
STEPHEN COLBERT

TWO GUYS WALK INTO A BAR. One's a nice Jewish boy from Lawrenceville, New Jersey, who went from college to busboy to stand-up comedian; the other a straight-arrow, private-school Southern kid with a degree from Northwestern in "the dramatic arts." They both end up delivering fake news on shows so wildly popular that they change the face of news, politics, and comedy. But that isn't even the story. Through the shock and tragedy of 9/11 and its aftermath, the heartfelt honesty of these guys emerged from behind the desks of *The Daily Show* and *The Colbert Report*, forging a friendship that can only be described as adorable—not a bromance, not buddies, not pals. These two guys giggle like five-year-olds in a sandbox, on and off the air, constantly trying to crack each other up, but also working to raise money and awareness for charities big and small. If it matters to one of them, it matters to both of them. There is nothing fake about that.

DOROTHY
+
TOTO

**JUST CLICK YOUR HEELS
THREE TIMES AND SAY,**

*"There's no place like home.
There's no place like home.
There's no place home."*

Chapter 2
THE UNEXPECTED

RUTH BADER GINSBURG

+

ANTONIN SCALIA

WOMEN'S RIGHTS
RBG 👍 Scalia 👎

SAME-SEX MARRIAGE
RBG 👍 Scalia 👎

VOTING RIGHTS ACT
RBG 👍 Scalia 👎

OPERA BUDDIES
RBG 👍 Scalia 👍

SOUVENIR SHOPPING
RBG 👍 Scalia 👍

NEW YEAR'S EVE FAMILY HANGOUTS
RBG 👍 Scalia 👍

> "*As annoyed as you might be about his zinging dissent, he's so utterly charming, so amusing, so sometimes outrageous, you can't help but say, 'I'm glad that he's my friend or he's my colleague.'*"

—RGB ON SCALIA

> "*If you can't disagree ardently with your colleagues about some issues of law and yet personally still be friends, get another job, for Pete's sake.*"

—SCALIA ON RBG AND THEIR LIFETIME APPOINTMENTS

And that, my friends, is how the world is meant to work.

MARILYN MONROE +

MARILYN'S SINGING COACH told her to listen to Ella's Gershwin records 100 times in a row if she really wanted to learn how to sing. So, America's sweetheart did just that. It was November 1954, in Los Angeles, when Marilyn got the true thrill of seeing her idol in person. No one would have predicted how close they would become—they hadn't yet shared their intimate secrets of troubled childhoods, struggling just to survive. It was Marilyn who got Ella her first BIG break at the Mocambo, the famous L.A. nightclub where Bogie, Bacall, Charlie Chaplin, and Clark Gable all held court, and the same famous haunt that refused to put the übertalented and

ELLA FITZGERALD

proudly voluptuous Black Fitzgerald onstage. Monroe promised the owner she would sit up front every night, with her celebrity pals like Sinatra and Garland. Every night, Ella sold out in front of her luminous friend. Still, despite her fame, the Queen of Jazz was forced to come into clubs through the kitchen or the back door. Again, MM stepped in. She famously refused to enter a Colorado club through the front door unless Ella was allowed to walk in beside her, like the royalty they were. Ella always remembered Marilyn's kindness: "I owe her a real debt," the First Lady of Song proudly proclaimed on more than one occasion.

HUNTER S. THOMPSON +
PAT BUCHANAN

SOME THINGS IN LIFE are just wonderful mysteries, amusing quandaries, and entertaining aperitifs. The kinship of Hunter S. Thompson and Pat Buchanan is certainly one of those things. Consider Buchanan—Nixon speechwriter and political adviser, and a devout Roman Catholic paragon of the political right who was so right of the right he was almost too right for the right. Hunter S. Thompson—Pitkin County sheriff candidate, father of Gonzo journalism, self-proclaimed action junkie, King of Fun, and proclaimer of "I do not advocate the use of dangerous drugs, wild amounts of alcohol and violence and weirdness—but they've always worked for me." They agreed on very little. They just liked each other. And Wild Turkey. Maybe it was an all-nighter at a Boston hotel drinking and, of course, debating political philosophies, as Nixon was making his comeback just before the 1968 New Hampshire primary, or Buchanan sneaking his oddball compadre onto a White House press corps plane. And who could accurately recall the two of them knocking back a cocktail or 12 poolside, at the Watergate, post-Watergate? Doubtful either of these two ideologues. But it all happened. That is on the record.

ANDY COHEN + JOHN MAYER

TO PARAPHRASE THE VOICEOVER from TV's *The Odd Couple: CAN* a big, tall, reformed womanizer, handsome straight guy and a shorter, square-jawed, cutey-patootey gay Dad be BFFs without dating each other? When they are both true-blue Deadheads who can feel the presence of Jerry Garcia surrounding them like a Real Housewife of Heaven, the answer is a resounding YES!

John welcomed his nightly phone buddy to his Montana haven so Andy could finish work on his last best-selling book. The two then piled into Mayer's bromobile for the ultimate Deadhead road trip to San Francisco for the 50th anniversary of the band. Along the way, Andy educated his dear friend on the true significance of Diana Ross, opening up yet another avenue for them to kvell over. To paraphrase (again) the classic Dead anthem "Sugar Magnolia": "He's got everything delightful / He's got everything I need."

MARK TWAIN + HELEN KELLER

"I CAN FEEL THE TWINKLE of his eye in his handshake," a 14-year-old Helen Keller proclaimed in the first of many touching meetings she had with the instantly enchanted Samuel L. Clemens, aka Mark Twain. The transformative occasion was a luncheon in honor of the young marvel, who had just arrived as a scholarship student at the Wright-Humason School for the Deaf in New York City. Twain was so impressed by "this miraculous creature, this wonder of all the ages" that he became her lifelong mentor. Though himself a bankrupt benefactor, he successfully implored his wealthy friends and fans to support Helen's education, including tuition at Harvard.

It was an unbroken mutual admiration society from the day they met. They shared a lifelong love of learning, wicked sense of humor, and confidence in their belief systems, which often ran counter to conventional wisdom. Literally and figuratively, they touched each other's souls.

MONICA LEWINSKY + ALAN CUMMING

WHEN YOU CAN BURY the image of the blue dress through the power of megakindness, self-awareness, true grit, and a 1,000-watt smile, you have to be that one-in-a-million lifetime friend we all dream about. Alan Cumming, the writer, actor, multitalented cabaret chameleon turned TV-star attorney, used his own bully pulpit to praise his good fortune in meeting this special goddess who has taught a generation what true empowerment means. Pop culture brought them together. Sensitivity, instinct, and goodness kept them close. Fierce loyalty and drive keep them moving forward. Lessons, people. Lessons.

KRIS
JENNER
+
JENNIFER
LAWRENCE

Keeping Up with K-Law, K-Maroney, Krinnifer, KrisLaw on E!

Don't question the universe that brought these cross-generation girlfriend besties together in the first place. Birthday celebrations, Girls' Nights, and cocktails in Kris's closet—a JLaw cameo on *KUWTK* is as real as it gets with this momager—it's sweet and silly all at once. And it's real. Don't question The Universe.

Chapter 3
HOLLYGOOD

THELMA + LOUISE

*Technically they were outlaws, but to women
of a certain age and girls forever after,
Thelma and Louise were freedom, courage,
the original ride-or-die best friends.*

THEY WERE WOMEN who, together, discovered their strength and beauty from within and reclaimed every bit of the control they had ceded to others. They built each other up, looked each other in the eye with joy and honesty, and dared to be bold. Side by side. Thelma and Louise ARE what friendship can and should be—glorious, liberating, soaring. Forever.

BETTE MIDLER + JULIANNE MOORE

LIFE IS FUNNY—and so are these two activators who fell deep and immediately in best-friend love when they met in the spring of 2019 on the set of the biopic *The Glorias*. Was it a meeting of the minds of these mission-driven mamas? Most BFF bonds are forged early and nurtured over time. But sometimes you just know when you know, and it wasn't long after these two met that they were dancing and laughing their way not just through the iconic Steinem's life, but also their own. Julianne schlepped her new bosom buddy to a junkyard clambake—appropriate for Midler, the Queen of Cleanup and founder of the New York Restoration Project, which has cleaned up outside spaces all around New York's five boroughs. Bette followed suit, soon presenting Julianne with her umpteenth award, recognizing her brilliance as both an actor and activist—in this case for mobilizing moms and families across the country to adopt smart gun reform at the 2019 Wall Street Journal Innovators Awards. While they take their causes seriously, they take their blossoming friendship as seriously as two spectacular power gigglers can.

BUSY PHILIPPS + MICHELLE WILLIAMS

FROM THE BANKS of *Dawson's Creek* to *Chicago* on Broadway, with a stop across the icy, windswept crevices of *Brokeback Mountain* and the suburban utopia of *Cougar Town*, much has been made about this 20-year love fest. These besties have always been a fan favorite, whether they're braving the hardest of times by each other's side, or dressing to the nines in vintage tulle and sequins, or sexy gamine columns swanning on red carpets hand in hand. Their polar-opposite public personas brilliantly shook up the looky-loos when the seemingly shy Michelle demanded equal pay and gender parity upon accepting her 2019 Lead Actress Emmy in front of a worldwide audience, with a beaming Busy unsurprisingly on her feet wildly supporting her brave BFF. They prefer porta-potty pictures to endless red carpet poses, and pasta parties to award galas. And they especially covet their special girl time. Michelle once told *USA Today* that Busy not only was the most selfless person she knows, but "you show up for all of us . . . and it's taught me everything that I know about being a friend."

DWAYNE JOHNSON +
KEVIN HART

ASK ANY TALK SHOW HOST or professional journalist what it's like to have a sit-down conversation with these brothers from other mothers and the best they might do is comment on the pair's sartorial splendor as they sit side by side in coincidentally matching outfits. Then let the games begin, with Johnson calling Hart his "snack-sized Denzel" and Hart trolling his giant-sized pal across any and every social media platform of the moment, with a full-on body-snatching photo or wig-wearing smackdown, attracting millions of fans' likes, comments, and booyahs.

Hulking Johnson and Little K are as close as two guys separated by more than a foot in physical stature can get, but the true depth of their friendship is undoubtedly measured by the nonstop public thrashing they give each other, all the while never crossing the cancellation line. When Kevin nearly died in a late 2019 car accident, his broken back didn't come close to Dwayne's nearly broken spirit monitoring his friend's recovery with the intensity of a true blood brother. You knew Kevin was on the mend when the sparring returned with a vengeance, each man determined to scale the highest peak of social media trolling. Who will ultimately measure up is a fast and furious battle of the besties.

HARRY
+
SALLY

HARRY: The first time we met we hated each other.

SALLY: You didn't hate me, I hated you. And the second time we met, you didn't even remember me.

HARRY: I did too, I remembered you. (A long beat.) The third time we met, we became friends.

SALLY: We were friends for a long time.

HARRY: And then we weren't.

SALLY: And then we fell in love.

SALLY: Three months later we got married.

HARRY: It only took three months.

SALLY: Twelve years and three months.

—NORA EPHRON,
WHEN HARRY MET SALLY

ANDY DUFRESNE +
RED REDDING

THEIR FRIENDSHIP BEGAN as a transaction. Red was the "guy who could get you things" at Shawshank State Penitentiary. Andy Dufresne's currency was intelligence, guile, and unrelenting hope. Stuck together in the most unnatural setting, these men were surrounded by despair, one man falsely imprisoned, the other filled with remorse but unable to see the light at the end of his long, dark sentence. They used prison yard rocks, library books, a Rita Hayworth poster, and the luxury of three bottles of beer to solidify their trust. What started as snippets of mess hall talks led to the sharing of secrets, one-man-to-another conversations—the kind real people have, but that people on the outside take for granted.

"Hope is a good thing, maybe the best of things, and no good thing ever dies." Words that Andy whispered to Red as he slipped away to freedom. Words that led Red to follow Andy to his ultimate dream. Friendship forever.

AIBILEEN CLARK + MINNY JACKSON

"YOU IS KIND. YOU IS SMART. YOU IS IMPORTANT." These are the three lessons Aibileen was determined to teach Mae Mobley, the last child she would raise and the most special, so Mae could survive in the world. Aibee's heart was as full as her mind was sharp. She was intent on writing her way out of Jackson, Mississippi, with her best friend and Jackson's best cook, Minny, by her side. Minny too was smart, kind, and soon to be important—with a toughness born from necessity, backed by a razor-sharp tongue that often crossed the boundaries of 1960s racially segregated Jackson. Not known to take anyone's shit, yet certainly able to serve it up cold. Minny and Aibileen triumphed over the deep-seeded racial caste system, as the most unlikely superheroes in a town of us versus them. Maybe we want to call them The Avengers, not The Help.

BUTCH CASSIDY +
THE SUNDANCE KID

WE KNOW THEM AS Butch and Sundance. Prolific turn-of-the-century bank and train robbers, who so confounded E. H. Harriman, the owner of the Union Pacific Railroad, with their nonviolent, gloriously successful rampage that he actually tried negotiating with them before turning the relentless Pinkerton lawmen on them in an intercontinental chase from San Francisco to Argentina, Texas to Chile, and ultimately, as we famously learn, gunning them down in Bolivia. The epic story as told by George Roy Hill made Robert Redford a movie star and solidified Paul Newman as box office catnip, despite what some of the more effete critics had to say. With wit, charm, and a natural verbal sparring that only happens when the chemistry is just right, Newman and Redford were forever Butch and Sundance to multiple generations of fans. Redford's ultimate tribute was made clear when he named the Sundance Film Festival after the brooding character developed by screenwriter William Goldman. Newman's love for the creative, childlike Butch cut just as deep, which he captured with the launch of the Hole in the Wall Gang Camp, created especially for children battling life-threatening illnesses. The legend and spirit of Butch and Sundance were meant to outlive the charming real-life desperados and their charismatic celluloid doppelgängers.

AUDREY HEPBURN +
GREGORY PECK

THEY MET ON the set of Audrey Hepburn's first film, *Roman Holiday*. Hepburn played a princess who fell in love with Peck's ink-stained newspaperman. Like his own character, Peck became completely enamored with Hepburn's brilliance and beauty, but after six months of shooting they came back to earth, bursting the bubble of audiences worldwide who fantasized that, unlike in the movie, they would remain bound by true love, together forever.

The good news for them, however, especially with Hepburn's chaotic Hollywood love life constantly scrutinized by gossipy friends and foes, was the lifelong friendship Peck and Hepburn forged. Trivia fanatics happily point out that Peck met his second (and last) wife on a studio publicity stop en route to Rome, and Hepburn met her first husband, Mel Ferrer, and father of her first child, at a post-filming party hosted by Peck at his home when they all returned to Los Angeles. Peck memorably paid tribute to Hepburn at the 1990 Golden Globes when he presented her with the prestigious Cecil B. deMille Award with the words "Elegant, graceful, radiant, incandescent . . . there just aren't enough adjectives. . . . Moviegoers are haunted by your looks, and enchanted by your performances. . . . You're a gift to us all."

B.J. Novak ✓ @bjnovak
♥ @mindy kaling

💬 730   ↩ 950   ♡ 1.2M   ⬆

Mindy Kaling ✓ @mindykaling
♥ @bjnovak soupsnakes 4ever

💬 850   ↩ 1.5K   ♡ 11.8M   ⬆

B. J. NOVAK +
MINDY KALING

HE IS GODFATHER TO HER KID. People are *obsessed* with their relationship status. There was a Tumblr blog dedicated to it; *Vulture* seemed to have a beat reporter assigned to them. Mindy and B.J. alternately have said they are besties, they aren't besties, they are family. HUH??? One writer dubbed it a "fromance" after they were paid $7.5 million to write a book about their relationship.

So why can't these two just be friends? They met post–Ivy League in 2004 because they are both really, really smart, excellent writing partners, acting colleagues, and onscreen/offscreen long-ago boyfriend/girlfriend for realz. He's from Newton, Massachusetts. She's from Cambridge, Massachusetts. They were kid geniuses and always adorable. Just when the noise dies down, they show up arm in arm at the exclusive post-Oscars *Vanity Fair* party, dressed to the nines, so beautifully platonic. Masters of Instagram posts, innocent Twitter teases, a casual cup of coffee captured by roving citizen paparazzi and BOOM!!! Are they, aren't they? Even Mindy and B.J. spar constantly about their relationship status. But they agree on two things: IT IS COMPLICATED and they are soup snakes.

MATT DAMON + BEN AFFLECK

SOUTHIES. BOSTON. *Good Will Hunting*. Oscars for both. The Red Sox. We all know the story. They grew up together—kind of the same, but different. One has that kid brother who always seems to be in the background. Close with their moms. Each now with a bunch of kids. One can't stay out of the tabloids, but you root for him. The other always lands on his feet, even if he occasionally trips over them or steps in it. He's the one with the million-dollar smile. And even if *Good Will Hunting* is as long ago for these two as Butch and Sundance is for the original Hollywood bromance, it just seems right to maybe one Sunday afternoon at Fenway or next week walking in Brentwood catch a glimpse of Damfleck or BenMatt, in rumpled T-shirts, Starbucks in hand, just sharing a laugh or cooking up a Kimmel payback.

Chapter 4
CHARACTERS

GRACE + FRANKIE

FRANKLY, BEING DUMPED by Sol and Robert was the saving grace for these stellar women. They showed each other (and any of us who bothered to pay attention) that you are never too old to stop, listen, and learn. Love comes at every age if you let it in. Hearts can be broken and words do matter, so stop, listen, and sometimes, just shhhh. Because grace is often more important than frankness when your very best friend is willing to spend her sunset years watching the sunset sitting next to you—no matter what.

LUCY + ETHEL

IF THELMA AND LOUISE had been born in the late 1950s or early 1960s, they would have been Lucy and Ethel. And just think: without grape-stomping-winemaking, Vitameatavegamin-selling, chocolate-candy-wrapping-assembly-line-working mayhem you would never have met WJM's Mary Richards and her bestie, Rhoda Morgenstern. Lucy and Ethel taught women how to get what they need and get men to listen a little harder without ever betraying each other. They also broke ethnic barriers without telling anyone— look America! A mixed-race marriage! English as a second language! And to this day, did we ever really know how old any of them were?

CAPTAIN KIRK +
MR. SPOCK

OPPOSITES ATTRACT and never was it truer than with the überlogical Vulcan Mr. Spock and the bold, audacious, often capricious Captain James T. Kirk. Their differences were the glue, the core strength of this originally short-lived yet eternally popular series that has spanned generations of TV, film, and universes beyond. They shared the captain's chair, sparred over a great love, were the target of Klingons and the evil Khan, shared true human emotions over an intergalactic biracial marriage between Spock's Vulcan father and human mother. On more than one occasion, they each risked their own life to save the other, because, in the end, human or Vulcan, womanizer or scientist, Roddenberry or Abrams, it was always and forever Kirk and Spock.

CRISTINA YANG + MEREDITH GREY

YOU'RE MY PERSON. Dance it out, hug it out. Cry it out. Ask no questions. Be there. When you are somebody's person you just know. It's that simple.

MARY + RHODA

You can't say Rhoda without Mary.

WHILE THEIR FRIENDSHIP had a slightly rocky beginning
with a misunderstanding over a third-floor studio apartment at
119 North Weatherly in Minneapolis, these two became unlikely
heroes for single working women everywhere. Mary, the naïve,
stammering Midwestern news producer at WJM-TV. Rhoda,
a streetwise, fast-talking Bronx-transplant window dresser at
Hempel's department store. Over the course of seven years, they
put power fashion, headscarves, and hat-tossing on the map.

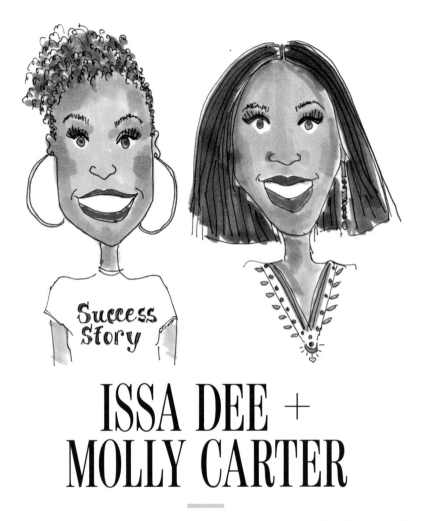

ISSA DEE + MOLLY CARTER

THE MOST ESSENTIAL things to know about Issa and Molly's friendship: (1) it is THE most important, enduring, dysfunctional, and honest love story of the series; (2) if you are expecting the stereotypical sassy black girl sidekicks, you will be waiting forever; (3) the beauty of Molly and Issa is the mundane, everyday, real-life twentysomething life they live—it is life, not TV life, not empirically every single black girl's life, just *their* life.

Malibu: remember that time we completely lost our shit with each other and then actually almost lost each other—MALIBU. I have you, I will call you out, but I have you. Now pass the chips, give me the remote, and get rid of that skanky orange romper.

MOLLY + AMY

WARNING: THIS IS ABOUT TEEN GIRLS!
SOS!! REQUIRED READING FOR BOYS

LET'S BE HONEST, if art imitates life imitates art, then decades of Hollywood movies have taught us that teen boys are, for the most part, jocky, horny, loud bad boyfriends, "bros before hoes," or nerdy, sensitive, friend-zoned geeks. And teen girls are one-dimensional, pretty OR smart, followers OR leaders, slutty OR righteous. *Booksmart's* Molly and Amy break the mold: they actually are actual real life. Not an imitation, finally! Here's the deal: calling all teenagers and listen up parents, you could learn something too. Adolescent girls, on the brink of adulthood, are layered: their friendships have depth, they are loyal, scared, joyful, filled with hope, refusal to regret, borderline codependent (oh please, this is what girls do for each other: stand.up and protect against all odds MALALA!). Except when they don't, and it is more devastating, more heartbreaking than any first romantic love—gay, straight, or otherwise. Molly and Amy aren't exceptional— they are magical—but they are typical. And that is what is magical.

Chapter 5
STYLEMAKERS

IRIS APFEL +
PERSONAL STYLE!

"If you're not interested, you're not interesting."

"You have to try it. You only have one trip. You've got to remember that!"

"If you don't know yourself, you'll never have great style. You'll never really live."

"The worst fashion faux pas is to look in the mirror, and not see yourself."

SHE'S GOT A BILLION OF THEM! Personal style, self-esteem, self-confidence, knowing who you are, and having just a little bit of fun with all of it. Iris Apfel shares the secret code: enjoy it! If it's not as clear as her oversized spectacles, Iris's bestie is inside Iris!

KARL LAGERFELD
+
CHOUPETTE

HIS CHOSEN PROFESSION and massive fame were the perfect mask for this impish, elusive artist. The designs were for his loyalists, the costumes for himself, to keep even his most intimate followers at bay, allowing this master of reinvention to evolve and disappear behind a creative curtain. Except from Choupette, the elegant Zhivago-like Birman cat, the pampered kitty who was the keeper of her master's secrets, and his closest confidante. Karl's gloved and jeweled hands were the instruments that magically expressed ideas, and the hands that lovingly held and stroked his beloved Choupette. Choupette famously arrived at chez Lagerfeld in 2011 as a visitor whose owner was away on two-week holiday. Lovingly seducing Mr. Lagerfeld, it was an immediate forever match. Never far from Karl's side during his life, Choupette adapted to her new glam lifestyle with ease, flying private, with her own Goyard china, two maids, and a bodyguard. Like Karl, Choupette showed an impressive work ethic, sitting for photo shoots, developing her own accessories line, and keeping up with her Instagram following. If art imitates life and Choupette imitates Karl, you can almost hear her purring his words from the 2007 documentary *Lagerfeld Confidential*: "I don't want to be real in other people's lives. I want to be an apparition. I appear, then disappear. I don't want to have reality in anyone's life, because I don't want it in mine."

*Karl's gloved and jeweled hands were
the instruments that magically expressed
ideas, and the hands that lovingly held
and stroked his beloved Choupette."*

DVF + BARRY DILLER

SHE IS A EUROPEAN ÉMIGRÉ, fashion icon, mother of the wrap dress, and godmother of the Statue of Liberty. A global philanthropist, DVF can often be found swimming for hours alongside her beloved luxury sailboat in the Mediterranean, contemplating which young female entrepreneur has made the greatest impact in sub-Saharan Africa or how to celebrate her beloved Barry's next birthday.

He was California born and bred, a media mogul who started in the legendary William Morris mailroom. Feared by competitors, idolized by loyalists, respected by everyone from social media billionaires to legacy media titans, "Killer Diller" is lovingly and ironically grounded by his wife, whom he married 27 years after becoming best friends. She saw beneath the tough guy image—his true shyness was a magnet; his bluster was for others. They both have a voracious appetite for living life to the fullest—different styles that have captured headlines and whispers and delivered everything from Match.com to the High Line. One thing they agree on: this is a couple that was meant to be.

RIHANNA + CARA DELEVINGNE

Party girls. Beautiful, sexy, enigmatic, giggling provocateurs. Paparazzi magnets.

WITH A DEEP, unrivaled connection sparked in the most public forum—a fashion show, cemented privately no matter where their superstar lives may take them. RhiRhi calls her a rock star, blessed to count her as one of her two or three special friends. Cara never misses a chance to swoon over @badgalriri— inspirational, pure love, an icon. Her friend.

BEFORE THEY MET more than 15 years ago, she was a self-proclaimed groupie, an überfan, taking advantage of privilege and position to travel across the globe to watch her tennis love rise or fall in a major final. For Anna Wintour, it was game, set, match when she was finally able to land her hero of the hard court for the 2017 Met Gala—her "other great passion." What was the spark that attracted the grande dame? His elegance. Roger didn't really know who Wintour was, but he trusted the mutual friend who introduced the pair. Over lunch at Pastis, the famed fashionista gathering place in New York's Meatpacking District, just before the U.S. Open so many Grand Slams ago, she peppered him with questions about his backhand, his strategy, and his mindset; he wanted to know everything there was to know about runway fashion, designers from Vuitton to de la Renta, who's who then and now. He dominated at lunch like on the court, and like all of Roger's formidable competitors, Anna succumbed. Match point: Roger won lunch, and while it is unclear who picked up the check, Anna remains a regular presence in the king's box.

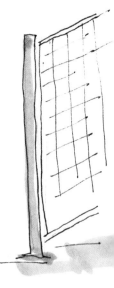

ANNA WINTOUR + ROGER FEDERER

STELLA McCARTNEY + LIV TYLER

"WALK THIS WAY" was definitely going to be the anthem for this next-gen dynamic duo, whose DNA would never allow them to just let it be as they cut their own patterns in life. Nothing called out these princesses of rock 'n' roll monarchies more than their show-stopping 1999 Met Gala debut: the same one-shouldered plain white cropped T-shirt, studded with ROCK ROYALTY across the front, one in casual hip huggers, one in a long satin skirt. The theme was Rock Style. Don't dare these daughters of kings. They were raised righteously.

MICK + KEITH

THEY'VE BEEN TOGETHER SINCE 1962. One thousand obituaries have been written. An equal number of reunions have followed. To paraphrase one of their greatest hits:

They keep trying and trying and trying and trying!

TARA LIPINSKI

$+$

JOHNNY WEIR

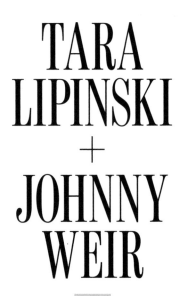

Sparkles, sequins, brocade, over-the-top fashion, hair and makeup, and that's just half of what makes NBC's #1 Winter Olympics broadcast team so popular.

TARA HAS CALLED JOHNNY her "partner in crime on and off camera for life," which was solidified when he stood up as a bridesman at her 2017 wedding. Johnny has already picked her as the godmother to any future child he may have and indelibly named her as his "please contact in case of emergency." They first bonded over Celine bags in an almost love-at-first-sight off-the-ice moment at the beginning of their broadcast career. The deal was sealed when they famously arrived at the airport heading to the 2018 Winter Olympics in South Korea with 13 oversized suitcases filled with coordinated outfits. Every piece was worn with no repeats. Hats included.

Chapter 6
CHANGEMAKERS

WARREN BUFFETT +
BILL GATES

PING-PONG, BRIDGE, golf, airport pickups. Dairy Queen.
You can't forget Dairy Queen. A day in the life of pretty much every
middle-class American family. But two of the richest men in America?
No way! Well, way! The first time they met, back in 1991, they talked
for 11 hours straight (who does that?). Especially when your mom
(Gates's) pretty much forced you to come to a dinner to meet her
friend Warren. The two things Buffett seems to treasure more
than money: time and friendship. Now that is rich.

Ballers. Divas.
Being the best you can be.

RuPAUL
+
MICHELLE VISAGE

BEHIND THE PINK, white, or platinum wigs, or the jet-black Jersey-girl-beauty-queen hair, are two fierce professionals, changemakers, and true "shapeshifters," in the words of RuPaul. More importantly—she is the girl behind the man, he has been there with decades of nonjudgmental devotion for one of his most well-respected judges. More than 30 years of laughter and love, protecting their outspoken values, learning together along the way.

NELSON MANDELA +
BISHOP DESMOND TUTU

ONE WAS ALREADY IMPRISONED for the brutal 27 years that would change both of their lives and impact people from Soweto and around the world. The other, studying to be a teacher and destined to become a different kind of messenger, enjoyed in the relative comfort of academia. A common fire and fight would bring them together, as brothers determined that neither of their lives and battles would be fought and won in vain. Tutu carried on the legacy of Madiba, his great friend, whom he proudly and without a hint of self-consciousness proclaimed to be the global icon of reconciliation and forgiveness.

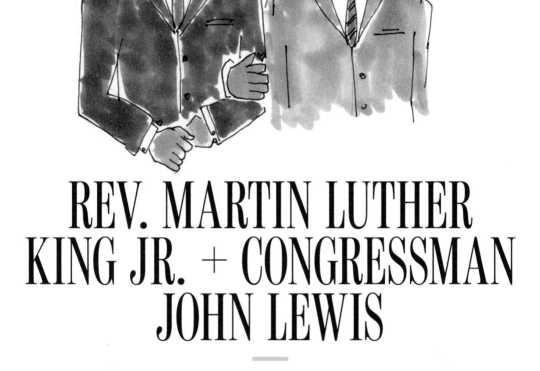

REV. MARTIN LUTHER KING JR. + CONGRESSMAN JOHN LEWIS

JOHN LEWIS WROTE a letter when he was 15 that changed his life.
Reverend Martin Luther King Jr. answered the letter, adding $15 for a bus
ticket. It changed both of their lives. They marched together, fought from separate
pulpits together, got into "good trouble" together. They both had a dream. Against
the odds, these men of action kept climbing the mountain of America's moral
compass in the ongoing, never-ending fight for civil rights. Thank you, Dr. King.
Thank you, Congressman Lewis. We will keep the dream alive.

SERENA + VENUS WILLIAMS

SERENA HAS WON her share of Grand Slams. Venus won them first, then helped pave the way to equal prize money for women at the Grand Slams, both Wimbledon and the French Open. Fashionable and fierce, these competitors, friends, sisters, and fighters were raised to be game changers on and off the court, Venus first, with her shadow, Serena, not far behind. Blow up convention: go to Fashion Week during U.S. Open week, say whaaat? Be friends with other women on the tour, wait, wait, then be *real* friends with each other—even when the little sister found her own self—no catfights, impossible! The lights shine bright no matter where Serena walks or whom she walks with these days, from the Royal Box to Queen Bey to Center Court in Queens, New York City. Her heart still belongs to her big sis and vice versa. "There's your average loyalty," Serena told *The New York Times Magazine* not too long ago, then there's Venus loyalty, which "for lack of a better word is mind-boggling." Deuce.

LIZZO +
THE TRUTH

What more could you ask for in a best friend than "Truth Hurts," her biggest hit and a global anthem to tough-love friendship? Not the Sam Smith, Jada Pinkett Smith, Missy Elliott new-fans friendship. Friendships solidified on the way up, like real-life Grammy shout-out friends Lauren (Sophia Eris) & Quinn (Wilson), Lizzo's tour mates/ collaborators/backbones. They know the truths, shared the hurts, and now get to celebrate the pure Hollywood moments with Melissa Viviane "Lizzo" Jefferson, like the time Justin Timberlake photobombed Queen Latifah's selfie with Queen Lizzo. OUCH!

EDIE WINDSOR + THEA SPYER

EDIE WAS A GAY DIVORCÉE and IBM tech exec who for
40 years was rarely without her long string of pearls and, more
importantly, her dancing and life partner, Dr. Thea Spyer. Married
for just two years before Thea lost her gritty battle against MS at
age 75, it was a $363,000 estate tax bill that ignited the final fire
Edie needed to go beyond till death do us part, all the way to the
Supreme Court to ensure that the love of her life was finally
recognized as her loving wife. Hell hath no fury . . .

GLORIA STEINEM +
MARLO THOMAS

THEY MET IN THEIR 20s, naïve, excited at the prospect of Thomas playing
Steinem as a Playboy Bunny in the TV movie about her *Show* magazine exposé.
Yet, as they say, the best laid plans of mice and men often go awry: when the
producer looked at the eager young women across from him, proclaiming, "Oh my
god, I don't know which one of you I want to f*%$ first!" it was a death knell for
the movie, but the birth of a thriving 50-plus-year bond between the star of *That
Girl*, which made Thomas into one of the world's most endearing feminists, and
Steinem, Ms. Foundation for Women cofounder, etc., etc.! Over these five decades,
both women have never stopped marching, raising awareness, and empowering
new generations of people to fight for equality for all—gender rights, equal pay,
issues that need a light, that require determined advocates. They are there for each
other for the big things, like weddings and illness, and the close family moments
like Thanksgivings. Raise a glass to this pair!

DIAN FOSSEY + DIGIT

NATURE KNEW THE POWER of this pair. The silverback Digit was born to protect the rainforest. Dian was born to protect Digit then, and all the Digits to come. In life and thereafter, the power of their love has overcome every obstacle to continue their protective reign.

Digit ❤ Dian. Dian ❤ Digit.

BILL MURRAY + DAVID LETTERMAN

PERHAPS IT'S THE pure Midwestern water, the down-to-earth roots that dissolved the host/guest desk protector between this arcane pair and moved them into the Friend Zone. Bill was Dave's first and last scheduled *Late Show* guest. A place of honor not to be ignored. Murray, famously elusive and quirky, is just as famously close with his Chicago-area extended family, so in 2003, when his friend Dave mentioned after one of Bill's 44 visits that baby Harry would be christened that weekend, Bill made sure the Murray family christening gown arrived about an hour later. Dave, with wife Regina and son Harry, has since returned the gesture, opening the gate to his Montana ranch and sharing a fishing pole or two on more than one occasion.

Chapter 7

PLAYMATES

BARBIE + KEN

CULTURAL ICONS. Always evolving. Forever Dreaming. Shero. They took a break (ahem, Rachel, Ross). He's on board. She can be on a Board. International superstars celebrating 60-plus years of success at work, at play. #Represent.

WOODY + BUZZ LIGHTYEAR

WHEN YOUR THEME SONG is "You've Got a Friend in Me," you learn to never give up on anyone. Woody, the giddyup, old-school rag doll, was Andy's loyal friend almost forever, overcoming his own early buzzing jealousies. And Buzz, the shiniest, newest toy on the block, learned that it wasn't always about being shiny and new; it's what's inside that counts.

ROCKY + BULLWINKLE

MOVE OVER DUDLEY DO-RIGHT, take a hike, Boris Badenov and your cunning spy girl, Natasha. If 1960ish America needs to be saved, it will be by this most unlikely pair of inseparable forest-dwelling antiheroes—may we present the ever resourceful, aerobatic Rocket J. Squirrel and his dense, good-natured cohort, Bullwinkle J. Moose.

SPONGEBOB + PATRICK

We have PRIDE every day, every month of the year:
SPONGEBOB SQUAREPANTS!

We love everyone in Bikini Bottom, LGBTQ+,
old, young, fish, squirrel, straight, or queer:
SPONGEBOB SQUAREPANTS!

Hey, Squidward, Mr. Krab, and Sandy Cheeks,
guess who's still yellow and squishy and wears matching
underwear? **SPONGEBOB SQUAREPANTS!**

UNDER THE SEA FOREVER!!
is this bubbly ace's loud and proud cheer!!

NEMO + DORY

THINK OZ'S SCARECROW and Rose from
The Golden Girls in the vast Australian oceans without
life jackets. Mix a little of *The Princess Bride*'s Fezzik with
the Cowardly Lion and you'll have the deep-sea version
of these two underfish who never stop swimming
against the current, where true family love awaits.

GUMBY + POKEY

YIN YANG, opposites attract, balance each other: all hallmarks of many everlasting friendships, even those formed from lumps of clay. Joyful, adventurous, a heartful hero, Gumby never allowed Pokey's cautious practicality to get in the way of a good escapade or discovery. Even the U.S. Marines shout "Semper Gumby!"

CHARLIE BROWN + SNOOPY

IN HIS ORANGE SHIRT with the giant zigzag design, Charlie Brown spent more than a lifetime seeking the approval of his dog, Snoopy, man's best friend. Or in this case, perhaps the reverse.

The authors struggled with the actual relationship and after much discussion settled upon the definition of best friend vs. employer and employee or owner and pet.

PEPPA PIG +
SUZY SHEEP

AT FOUR YEARS OLD, these two power pre-Ks are already destined for greatness: Peppa has been dubbed bossy; they've both been labeled smart, cheeky, and chatty, yet care more about using their voices and participating, sitting quietly, following not leading; they are exuberant muddy puddle jumpers, curious and caring. They lead hand in hand.

WINNIE-THE-POOH +
CHRISTOPHER ROBIN

"We will be friends until forever,
just you wait and see."

—A. A. MILNE
(WHY TRY TO IMPROVE UPON
PERFECTION ;))

Chapter 8

ARTISTES

ERIC CLAPTON + GEORGE HARRISON

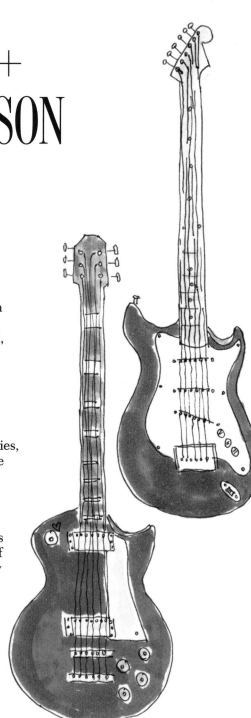

NOT EVEN "IT WAS THE 60s" could properly explain the strength of this friendship. Perhaps Harrison's later-in-life devotion to the Hindu concept of *maya,* of cosmic illusion, what Beatles fans, or aficionados, might call extreme "Ob-la-di-ob-la-da-ism" comes close. You know, life goes on, bra, or the concept of "get over it!" Whatever the label, Eric Clapton and George Harrison's friendship was forged around their blind devotion to their epic guitar talents and survived a nearly 20-year span of literal sex, drugs, and rock 'n' roll, not to mention the interruptions of broken hearts, broken bands, and broken marriages to the same woman. Clapton played guitar solo on Harrison's song "While My Guitar Gently Weeps" on the Beatles' legendary White Album, while Harrison paid tribute to Clapton's notorious sweet tooth on the double record's song "Savoy Truffle." Infidelities, divorces, addictions, rehab—it's no joke—yet there was George at the wedding of his ex-wife to his best friend, dubbing himself the husband-in-law: "I'd rather she be with him than some dope."

The marriage dissolved in 1988, but Harrison and Clapton's friendship endured, with Harrison's spirituality guiding Clapton's demons to a place of peace and happiness. At the one-year anniversary of Harrison's death, Clapton organized The Concert for George memorial in 2002 at London's Royal Albert Hall, bringing together musicians and spiritual masters to pay tribute to the elder brother he never had, while his own guitar gently weeped.

DAVID BOWIE +
LOU REED

UNLIKEABLE. CRASS. EGOMANIACAL. MISOGYNISTIC.
Words assigned on a regular basis to Lou Reed, prior to some
mellowing in the twilight Laurie Anderson years. Beautiful. Elegant.
Otherworldly. *Au fait.* Bowie's yin to Reed's yang. Nevertheless,
and barring the substance-induced punch-in-the-face incident, it does
seem that Bowie and Reed were inseparable, creative comrades,
the student becoming a near equal to his master.

PATSY CLINE +
LORETTA LYNN

IT WAS BRIEF, deep, heavenly. A car crash brought them together,
a plane crash couldn't destroy a kinship that lasted beyond a lifetime. How
do you repay the angel who literally gave you the shirt off her back and the
panties from her travel bag? Patsy was Loretta's mentor, guardian angel,
inspiration, and friend. Well, you repay her the only way that makes any
sense if you're country music royalty: you sing. You don't fall to pieces or get
crazy. Loretta wasn't going to waste the lessons she learned about strength,
empowerment, standing up for the next in line. She named one of her
twins Patsy and kept Cline's music alive, the greatest tribute of all.

CARRIE FISHER
+
PENNY MARSHALL

THESE TWO WOMEN, both born in October, who shared wit, heart, a preference for privacy, and unrivaled show business pedigree, also shared a friendship that Marshall once observed survived the years of all of their marriages combined. They met on the late 1970s party scene, but it wasn't a "will you hold my hair" friendship—they got each other. They clicked. Sure, Jack Nicholson, Robin Williams, Anjelica Huston, and Meryl Streep were regulars at the infamous joint birthday bashes. Names like Affleck and Kidman were considered newbies, Bowie and Iman crashers.

Their fondness for their beloved opposite coasts—Marshall's New York roots recalled her, while Fisher stayed adjacent to her driveway neighbor, mother Debbie Reynolds in L.A.— might have separated them geographically, but as any A-list behind-the-scenes writer/ director/actor worth her salt will attest, not even a country would ever come between them.

PRINCE
+
JANELLE
MONÁE

**SHE WAS BORN
TO BE A STAR,**
the shining light in
her proud, extended
Kansas City family.
She practices the only
religion that makes
sense to her: love.
Confusion, brilliance,
lights, camera, action—
enter music's most
ethereal superstar to
make sense of it all.
To the world he is,
was, will always be
Prince. To Monáe,
he was the king. The
voice in her head, the
inspiration in her heart,
her pen, her internal
computers, whatever
her instruments of
the moment. His trust
was not to be wasted.
The phone calls at all
hours have stopped,
but the love between
them lives on and the
journey continues.

FRAN LEBOWITZ +
TONI MORRISON

SO MANY THINGS in common, not so much. Fran is a dyed-in-the-wool New Yorker. Toni, not so much—she couldn't remember uptown from downtown, would take a cab five blocks to eat. Walk? Ha! Fran holds a grudge. Cannot understand why or how you turn the other cheek. Be the bigger person? Let it go? NEVER! Toni, not so much—forgiveness was her nature, compassion her middle name. Figuratively she walked a mile in even a frenemy's shoes. Fran had a style, more like a uniform: jeans or black pants, blazer, white tailored shirt. Toni had style; she loved clothes, a pop of color, a Judith Leiber bejeweled bag, a sweeping cape. But what they had in common filled a lifetime of memories. These ladies had fun. F-U-N. FUN. Going out on the town fun. Reading trashy tabloids fun. Never missing dessert, McDonald's, or birthday parties with presents FUN. Who but a prolific Nobel Prize winner in literature and one of the most widely admired authors who published only four books would rent a limo for a night of bingo at the casinos in Connecticut?

GERTRUDE STEIN + PABLO PICASSO

She was the ultimate American in Paris. An expat, ex–med student, and bohemian newbie art collector, Stein used her salon and support of the Euro avant-garde modernists to launch the careers of Henri Matisse and, of course, emerging artiste Pablo Picasso. Of all the women in Picasso's life, Stein was the most perplexing, his muse and confidante. They were as much competitors as compadres: Stein, the writer, often reminding people of her very own genius, often to the peril of her own relationships; Picasso, more charming, more controlling, always the painter first, writer later, allowing his genius to be praised by others. Her celebrity was indisputable, his genius was indisputable, their bond fraught but indestructible. *Sacré bleu! Quelle dramatique!*

ARETHA FRANKLIN + SMOKEY ROBINSON

R-E-S-P-E-C-T. What it really meant to these musical icons, Detroit's best and brightest, was L-O-V-E. They were each other's longest, deepest friendship, a bond that began when Aretha was five and Smokey was eight. She moved into the neighborhood from Buffalo, living in what seemed like a mansion with her father, the Reverend C. L. Franklin, and a pack of siblings. Aretha may have been a tomboy, but Smokey knew she was a queen from the beginning—this little girl could sing! When it got real, Smokey stayed in and with Motown; young Aretha went to New York. Nothing really changed. Their friendship just became long phone calls every night. There was a serendipitous one-time appearance on *Soul Train* in 1979. It is hard to believe these two identical spirits never recorded together. But they talked and talked and talked. It was rarely music talk. No, it was children, marriage, recipes. Family. Yes. Money. Yes. R-E-S-P-E-C-T. Yes. For communities, for the generations that followed them. At her funeral in August 2018, surrounded by choirs, actors, family, a President and First Lady, there was her longest friend. As far as Smokey is concerned, "She will always be the Queen."

MILEY CYRUS + ARIANA GRANDE

High ponies. Booming voices. High style.
Stunning vocals. Cutie pies, talented beyond their years.

THEY TWEET, GRAM, SNAP, live their lives in public, their friendship on screens like regular Gen-Z influencers, normal millennials. Their university is onstage, backstage, different campuses, same studies. They are innocently reckless, entertain high-octane romances, explosive breakups. In public. Girls being girls being girls doesn't get any better, unless you can put it to music too!

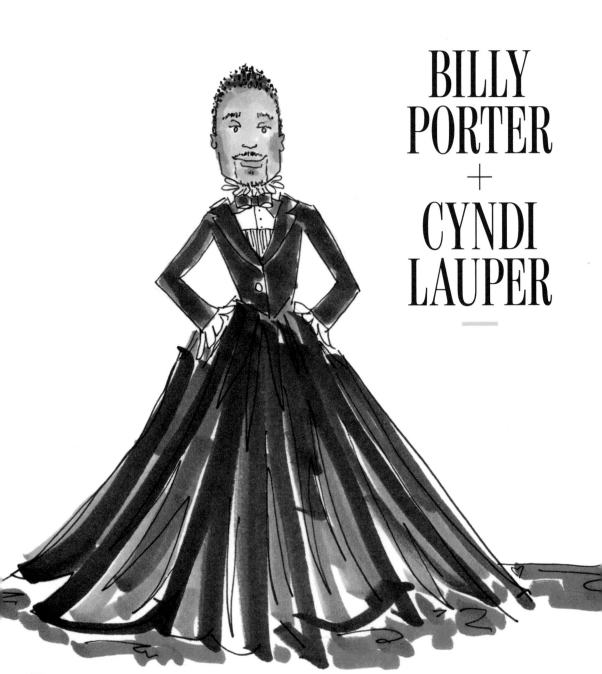

BILLY PORTER
+
CYNDI LAUPER

HE "KNEW" HER
long before *Kinky Boots*
and Lola changed his life.
She *had* to find him once
she heard him. Billy Porter
is on the record saying
that *Kinky Boots* freed his
femininity, helping him
find his true colors. Cyndi
Lauper discovered long
ago that you have to love
yourself—first, always—
as a person and the
artistry will follow. Once
these freed spirits came
together in 2012, working
on the multi-Tony-Award-
winning musical, they
knew it was going to be
a forever thing. Pray
tell, it looks like offstage,
surrounded by a bevy of
besties or alone, these two
just wanna have fun ;)

Chapter 9
SQUADS

EVELYN + NINNY, IDGIE + RUTH

THIS SQUAD OF FIERCE, loving women needs a reboot! Or, as the loving storyteller Ninny might suggest, refry these green tomatoes! Between the beatings onscreen and the shushing offscreen, it's time to blow the whistle at the Whistle Stop Cafe. Ninny teaches Evelyn to celebrate her most important relationship: with herself, to become her own true friend. TOWANDA! As she learns to love herself, Evelyn falls in love with Idgie and Ruth, the purest love story she has ever known. As pure as honey from an old bee charmer on a perfect summer day. Idgie and Ruth's love story is built upon Idgie's abiding sense of justice and intolerance of cruelty and Ruth's eternal optimism. With a baby to be raised between them, Ruth's message to Idgie from the Book of Ruth sealed their together forever: "Whither thou goest, I will go; and where thou lodgest, I will lodge: thy people *shall* be my people, and thy God my God."

OUISER, TRUVY, M'LYNN, CLAIREE, ANNELLE + SHELBY

THESE STEELY BUT GRACEFUL WOMEN are guided by tradition, friendship, and loyalty with an allowable amount of eccentricity. And a little Cajun spice. Never come between them. Never question their character. Do not be fooled by their affinity for shades of blush and bashful. And do not ever, *ever* underestimate this Southern six-pack's will or strength. As Shelby so emphatically proclaimed, "I would rather have thirty minutes of wonderful than a lifetime of nothing special."

CHANDLER, JOEY, ROSS, RACHEL, PHOEBE + MONICA

"I'LL BE THERE FOR YOU" should be the theme song for these best friends. Oh wait, it is! The actors all met for the first time at the table read for the iconic sitcom a generation has grown up on and new ones have discovered. Through haircuts, marriages, boyfriends, pregnancies, and weekly tabloid fodder, this group has never been on a break—they've truly refined the meaning of best friends. They are there for each other when the rain starts to pour, cause they've been there before and pretty much seem like they'll always be there—forever!

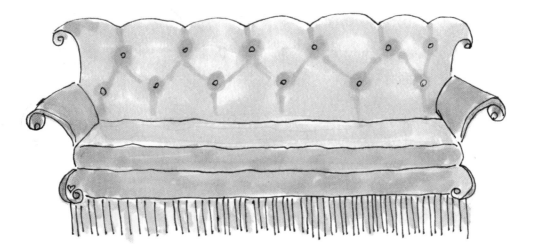

JERRY, ELAINE, GEORGE + KRAMER

CHOCOLATE BABKA almost broke them up. A puffy shirt nearly destroyed them. Shrinkage threatened George's already precarious self-image, and man-hands, envelope glue, face-painting, and a female body part were all causes for broken relationships. While Elaine had to live with the shame of shutting down the Soup Nazi and Kramer nearly disrupted the ocean's balance with an errant golf ball, this misfit band of brothers and an ex-flame survived, in spite of themselves, to ultimately succeed as the Masters of Their Domains ☺

HARRY POTTER, RON WEASLEY + HERMIONE GRANGER

IS THREE ALWAYS A CROWD?
Not when you lose your parents as a
child and your friends are your family.
In the magical and chaotic world
of Harry Potter, with its chambers
of secrets and the fate of the world
hanging in the balance, loyalty, bravery,
trust, and love are literal lightning rods
that define what Harry receives from
his friend-for-life Ron Weasley and the
bright, take-no-prisoners Hermione.
She's the bossy sister who, despite
constant nagging, was always there
to save Harry's life—hellooo death
of Voldemort, creating Dumbledore's
Army, and basically saving them
all during the Horcrux Hunt. With
no Hermione, not even magic saves
these guys. Ron and Harry, in spite
of each other (good decision-making
aside—ahem, the prison of Azkaban),
were miserable when they temporarily
abandoned one another, proclaiming
aloud they were family forever. Family
by choice, nothing can really come
between this threesome—and, just in
case . . . *"Expecto Patronum!"*

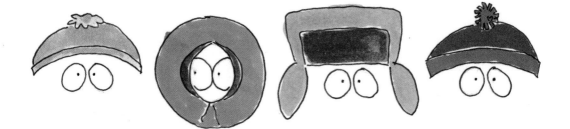

CARTMAN, KENNY, KYLE + STAN

WHEN YOU LIVE IN SOUTH PARK, Colorado, arguably the most screwed-up place in America, finding your boys is an imperfect but necessary journey to survive elementary school. Enter The Boys. Kyle and Stan, the moral compass of the whole fourth grade. Kyle's crazy computer skills are otherworldly. He's proudly Jewish, a tad too honest for a nine-year-old. Yep, he's the guy who fesses up to TPing houses around town. Fortunately, he's also a major ninja warrior, helpful in his ongoing battles against his nemesis, Cartman. Stan, a mostly normal fourth grader, has crazy athletic skills—from football and hockey to dance and even *Guitar Hero*. His ego can become insufferable to The Boys, even BFF Kyle. In these shaky moments, he famously turns to "one voice he can rely on, wondering . . . what would Brian Boitano do?" It's all about survival in South Park. Cartman, undeniably racist, sadistic, sociopathic, narcissistic, and greedy, is the antihero. His devotion to the town's poorest kid, Kenny, began as a mutual bond over vices but morphed to genuine affection as Kenny watched Cartman's fourth-grade psychosis become dangerously mature. Contrary to the web of complexities of typical grade school-friendships, Kenny's lack of pretension enabled him to cement relationships with this entire crew, a superpower that exceeds his ability to defy death, which is basically inexplicable considering a 23-year running theme of "Kenny dies." Kenny's the allegory. He may be the poorest, but he'd do anything for his friends, even die for them, which makes him the richest.

EDDIE MURPHY, DAVE CHAPPELLE, TRACY MORGAN + CHRIS ROCK

THEY GATHERED ONSTAGE for Eddie Murphy's triumphant return to *Saturday Night Live* on December 21, 2019, and for the live and viewing audience, it was one of the great monologue moments. For Chappelle, Morgan, and Rock, it was the ultimate way to publicly thank their guy. These superstars, all icons in their own right, share something very special: Murphy. He inspired them to become comedians, and along the way they have become fast friends. Like finding the right timing for the perfect joke, actually being together, face-to-face, for this brotherhood is a nearly impossible feat with the geographic challenges of living in four different states, constant touring, and, you know, life (bundle of kids, a divorce here and there, you know, life). They all have personal Eddie Murphy reminiscences, but Tracy Morgan, who takes little for granted these days, having survived a near fatal highway accident in 2014, captured it best, remembering back to his first year on *SNL* in 1996 when Murphy invited him for a walk just to tell him how proud he was of the young comic. A grateful Morgan recognized the importance of the moment, saying, "Eddie, thank you for keeping the door open for me."

FRANK SINATRA, DEAN MARTIN, SAMMY DAVIS JR., JOEY BISHOP + PETER LAWFORD

GLAMOUR AND MOVIE STARS, with a dash of swagger, a jigger of glitz, a shot of cool. Wrap it in diamonds, slip on a tux, chill a perfect martini. It's 1960 at the Hollywood home of Bogie and Bacall, and the Rat Pack is just about to be born. Surrounded by the likes of Elizabeth Taylor, Spencer Tracy, Katharine Hepburn, Robert Mitchum, and Ava Gardner, this devilish quintet rounded out what could only be described as a block party on steroids every weekend, like the last men standing—barely. Then Vegas happened. With the silky-voiced crooners formally dubbed "The Rat Pack" on the marquee at the Sands Hotel and Casino, and voilà! The original boy band. They headlined to sold-out crowds onstage, then dazzled fans offstage with antics led by chief party boy Martin. The fun continued when movie offers started rolling in, and the Rat Packers became royalty starring in films from *Ocean's 11* to *Robin and the 7 Hoods*. They hit the pause button when Kennedy politics miffed Sinatra and replaced Lawford with Bing Crosby, but the standard for cool and glamour had already been set, an era frozen in time.

SIMONE BILES, GABBY DOUGLAS, ALY RAISMAN, LAURIE HERNANDEZ + MADISON KOCIAN

Powerful. Inspirational. Irrepressible. Disciplined.

THEN THEY FOUND THEIR VOICES. Then they changed the world. Way beyond friendship, beyond Olympic gold. They are Mount Rushmore Next Gen. El Capitanne sounds good! !!!!!

QUEEN ELIZABETH + CORGIS

"IT'S A DOG'S LIFE" takes on a whole new meaning when you are talking about one of the thirty corgis that Queen Elizabeth II has counted among her very best friends since 1933. Beginning with family puppies Dookie and Jane, it was Susan whom 18-year-old Princess Elizabeth was first able to call her own. Susan joined the queen on her 1947 honeymoon with Prince Philip and was the matriarch for every one of the royal pups that followed. Holly, Monty, and Willow famously costarred with the queen in the 2012 Olympic opening ceremonies video with Daniel Craig; Holly and Willow were featured on the cover of *Vanity Fair* in 2016.

Queen Elizabeth tended personally to the corgis' royal menu, prepared daily by a dedicated gourmet chef; made individual Christmas stockings for each best pooch; and selected custom-made elevated wicker sleeper baskets to ensure no chilling drafts touched these royal bellies. In return, her loyal pets kept her secrets with no fear of leaks or betrayal. And their royally refined radar wasn't afraid to occasionally nip the hands of potential frenemies. When QE2 laid her last beloved Willow to rest in 2018, the silence of no more yapping could be felt throughout Buckingham Palace, the stiff upper lip tradition of calm and carry on replaced by a noticeably bereaved monarch. A Queen without her only true court running along beside her.

Chapter 10
GOODIES

COCO CHANEL SAID IT BEST:

"I only drink champagne on two occasions: when I'm in love and when I'm not!"

CHAMPAGNE + CAVIAR

JAMES BOND USED IT to judge a man's character: "Any man who drinks Dom Pérignon '52 can't be all bad." Jay-Z, Lady Gaga, Kanye, and Queen were all savvy enough to sing about what 17th-century monk Dom Pérignon proclaimed as "tasting the stars." Chilled to perfection, small bubbles, crisp, pink or white—it is the elixir of the gods and dream makers from Grace Kelly and Cary Grant to Elizabeth Taylor and Richard Burton, Beyoncé to Leo. It ushers in the New Year or a new baby, celebrates the Super Bowl champs or the first college graduate in the family. And perfection is only achieved when paired with the PB&J of the elite: beluga, sevruga, osetra caviar—take your pick, but never ever pick it up with anything but a mother of pearl spoon, perhaps smooth bone. Touch it with metal and *poof!* you have destroyed the precious gem of the Caspian Sea, trashed the integrity of this crunchy, salty delicacy. Fantasy destroyed, worse than Cinderella at 12:01!

PEANUT BUTTER + JELLY

THIS ISN'T BRAIN SURGERY: five minutes, anytime, day or night, not a lot of cash, and you're starving? What says perfection better than Welch's grape jelly spread evenly on one slice of fresh white Wonder Bread? Waiting patiently, just tickling right up against my crust, is another equally fresh slice of Wonder Bread, ready for smooth, rich Skippy peanut butter to be swirled and spread, edge to edge. Before too long, the pieces are flipped evenly together and VOILÁ! PERFECTION! If sandwiches got married and you celebrated their anniversary in seconds, not years, then PB&Js would be the first married sandwich. Do not ask who is the bride!

MAC + CHEESE

COLLEAGUES? FRIENDS?
Noodle on it.

CHIPS + GUAC

YOU ORDER GUACAMOLE AND CHIPS, but who are we kidding: we all just want the chips. Say what you want, but the guacamole is the healthy beard, the "I love avocado" cover, the this needs more heat, see I try "new" foods cover for glorified snack food. You *never* run out of guac first. Okay, maybe sometimes you do. Let's get it chunky. Maybe try the mango salsa/ghost pepper/habanero/coffee guacamole. Never mind. WE JUST WANT THE CHIPS!

PIZZA + ANYTHING!

HEY, COME OVER HERE. You wanna talk about billions of besties when it comes to food? No contest. Anytime, day or night, hot or cold, deep-dish or thinny-thin. Round unless you are in Chicago or Detroit and then rectangle. By the slice, a whole pie. A kid's birthday party, living on campus/off campus/just moved out/just moved in/just moved back. How about a plain, just bubbly with cheese and tomato sauce, or throw some stuff on it—classic stuff, maybe basil for a nice margherita, or pepperoni for the kids, mushrooms for the vegetarians, sausage, prosciutto, garlic, peppers, onions, extra cheese. Oooohhh, you're a fancy one, with your brick oven, having friends over out by the pool. Pizza with clams, shrimp, short rib (of course you made the brisket on the outdoor smoker). I don't love pineapple, but, then again, when you're serving the best friend of all food, anything goes. Including . . . wait for it . . . bianca, no sauce, four-cheese only. Your best foodie friend in the world says VIVA LA PIZZA! VIVA LA PIZZA!

SPAGHETTI + MEATBALLS

EVERYONE HAS A STORY, a favorite recipe, their grandmother/grandfather's/aunt's/don't start with me, best restaurant, finest you'll ever have. I promise you, did I tell you not to start with me, just trust me, seriously, just try this one. This one. It never ends. Songs have been written, families have feuded, lawsuits have been filed. THAT, my friends, is how much love there is between spaghetti and meatballs.

TOMATO + MOZZARELLA

FEEL LIKE A SALAD TONIGHT?
I'm plattered.

FEEL LIKE PIZZA?
I was thinking just us for a change.

BLT + TOAST

A LIGHT SWIPE OF MAYO. A side of chips. A deep breath. Exhale. Twenty minutes of simple comfort and peace. Go ahead world. Keep spinning. Lunch is my best friend.

CHICKEN
+
WAFFLES

WHO SERVED IT FIRST and who serves it best is a loud and proud classic North vs. South debate that stretches from the seventeenth-century Pennsylvania Dutch settlers, to German settlers in Virginia in the 1800s smothering thick gravy over their chicken and waffles Sunday breakfast, to the 1930s Well's Supper Club in Harlem. Atlanta's own Gladys Knight and Brooklyn-born Biggie Smalls elevated chicken and waffles to a whole new level, moving it out of the ritual Sunday family dinner and into the mainstream. The kind of artery-clogging goodness that we all guiltily crave, slurp, and order "only on special occasions," "because they're from out of town," "since we have to celebrate," or "seeing it's been that kinda week." Find an excuse, any excuse. And then find a bib and a friend. Because what is indisputable in the crunchy, delicious sweetness when you combine these seemingly disconnected breakfast and dinner treats is, no matter the roots, chicken and waffles need to be shared with a friend.

BACON
+
EGGS

THE BEST THING about bacon and eggs is their flexibility. The smell of bacon wafting through the air, whether it's crispy, just a little browned, slightly curled, or nearly burned with a hard crunch—that completely intoxicating, come-one-come-all inviting aroma—stands up well to whatever egg decides to slide next to it on that warm, anytime-day-or-night plate. Dry scrambled, sunny side up, broken and over, a perfectly timed soft-boiled, a jammy—bring it on! Large, jumbo, organic, free-range. Cozy up. It is breakfast 24/7 with this BFF combo. Just remember to serve it up fresh and hot. Toast is optional.

CANDY HEARTS + SWEET WORDS

FOR 154 YEARS, Candy Hearts, or conversation hearts as they were known back in 1866, have sweetened the world with pithy phrases such as "HOW LONG SHALL I HAVE TO WAIT? PLEASE BE CONSIDERATE" and loving coos like "PLEASE BE MINE." Conjure up the joyful feeling whenever you received even a single, sugary-flavored heart or the sheer delight of a card filled with hearts of sweet words and phrases. We hope our 140-ish pages of Sweet Words fill you with the same warm glow. XOXO

ACKNOWLEDGMENTS

FROM THE OUTSET, we envisioned that creating *Billions of Besties* would be a delightful adventure, a labor of love and whimsy. Clearly, the idealistic musings of first-time author/creators. It remains all of those things, but with a newfound respect and admiration for the layered, complex, byzantine process it takes getting from sketchbook and research notes to the bookshelf. We want to thank the besties brigade for their inspiration, guidance, and attention to detail, for their taste, humor, knowledge, and newfound friendships is deep. You are on our list forever.

Thank you to Peggy's besties Jennifer Hawkins + Robin Wong for the adventure in Santa Fe that lit the spark + illuminated the path for creating art again, for their unwavering support and for Jennifer's introduction to Theresa DiMasi at Tiller Press.

To Polly Panosh + Stuart Rossmiller's loving generosity in opening their delightful Door County home to Peggy and allowing her to turn it into her studio to complete the illustrations for this book during shelter-in-place. And to the rest of her amazing family for their unbridled love and support.

Susie must thank Leslee Dart for the seminal cup of coffee and most profound reposado tequilas, three limes, straight up, with Amanda Lundberg and Bill O'Dowd that cleared the path both reigniting creativity and resolve.

To mom, Marilyn Arons, for her endless gratitude and pride. Sandy Arons, whose love of life, family, and sense of integrity was always shining from above. To Kayla Pressman—Auntie, this writer has no words.

Thank you, Team Besties: Scott Felcher, your legal guidance and wisdom wrapped in humor cared for us in a billion ways. Cheers to Jenny Lerner and Kate Fraser; who better to help share our stories than our very own besties?

No two first-time creatives could ever ask for a better team to helm this complex web of a process better than the talented and innovative crew at Tiller Press.

Our heartfelt gratitude to Theresa DiMasi, our chief steward, for saying yes to this book; you kept us on course, pushing us forward with enthusiasm and championing it and us every step of the way.

Thank you to Anja Schmidt for her wisdom, good taste, and guidance to get us to the finish line. To Patrick Sullivan and Matthew Ryan for their patience and artful sense of style, and Hannah Robinson for her energy and creativity.

And, to the passionate Tiller Press sales team, the network of booksellers—big and small—the gift shops, retailers, and YOU, dear reader—for believing that celebrating best friends is a wonderfully positive and worthwhile thing to share. . . . x a billion. We thank you.

To the people, characters + things we befriended in this book, thank you for your fascinating and simply exceptional friendships.

ABOUT THE CREATORS

PEGGY PANOSH has carved a unique dual career path as both a highly respected marketing expert + illustrator. With more than 30 years in media and entertainment, Peggy has worked with some of the most prolific celebrities, namely Oprah, and world-renowned events from the Grammys to the Super Bowl, creating memorable moments for audiences all along the way. As a passionate traveler, having explored more than 70 countries, Peggy's love for creating art was ignited during one of her many global adventures. Her illustrations capture the heart and spirit of the people, places, and moments that touch her soul. In fact, if you look very closely at her drawings, you will find a teeny little heart in each one. Peggy's illustrations have been seen on *CBS Sunday Morning*, and she was a featured artist at Soho House's Ludlow House in New York City. She splits her time between Brooklyn, New York, and Madison, Wisconsin. More of her work can be seen at peggypanosh.com

SUSIE ARONS is a strategic communications adviser, working with some of the most recognized names in entertainment, lifestyle, and media. She has honed her writing skills penning billions of messages throughout her 30-plus-year career; some people might say she has also been a professional bestie to some of the besties in the business, including Netflix, HBO, Color Force, Marlo Thomas, *The Defiant Ones*, St. Jude Children's Research Hospital, A24, Refinery29, Child Mind Institute, *The Hunger Games*, Amazon Studios, BMW, Focus Features, Starz, AMC Networks, *West of Memphis*, Apple Music, Jimmy Iovine, Sundance TV, Jonah Hill, The Orchard, the Radio City Christmas Spectacular, and the Tribeca Film Festival. Inspired every day by her colleagues or poolside with her treasured circle of friends and family, Susie learned early to lead with her heart, be smart, and always keep the joy.

POLLY STUART CIEL LEO JENNIFER JOHN HARRISON MADELINE JERI
JENNIFER JON JEMMA BECKETT ROBIN BILL TRACY ERIKA ALESSAND
MARY (SISTER SLEDGE) JULIE JILL MICHAEL HARRIET JONAH EMMA RO
BOB ANN KRISTEN GAIL KATHY TOM PENELOPE DEEPAK FARLEY MICH
KATIE KERITH HILLARY THERESA BILL CARRIE CONNIE PAM NICOLE S
PETE DEIRDRE JOE SEANA WYATT AL MAUREEN JENNY JOE KATE LI
LUCY SCOTT THERESE LINDSAY MEL RICHIE JON WENDY PATTI SCOT
MILLIE AUNT RUTH SUSANNE RALPH CHANEL CHERYL MICHAEL KATIE S
FREIDA MARLO JEANEANE LIZA ZOE JIM KATHRYN SALLY JIM DEB A
NICKI CAREN SAMANTHA SHELLEY POLLY STUART CIEL LEO JENNIF
LEO LEEANN LOIS RICHARD SUSIE JENNIFER JON JEMMA BECKETT
ALI PETER ELI TIM SUSAN MELISSA MARY (SISTER SLEDGE) JULIE JI
PAISLEY NAOMI PAUL MARNIE JOANNE BOB ANN KRISTEN GAIL KAT
AMY MICHELLE MEL JENNA TERRY SONA KATIE KERITH HILLARY TH
JEREMY SANFORD MARILYN KAYLA MURPHY PETE DEIRDRE JOE SEAN
MIKE SUE CINDY JULIE LISA JONATHAN TIM LUCY SCOTT THERESI
STELLA CAROLYN ANDREW EMILY BARBARA FRED MILLIE AUNT RUTH
EDDIE CHERYL PILAR JIMMY KEN AUNT ESTHER RACHEL FREIDA MARLO
CHERYL TAHRA GARY SHARLEEN TONY DAVID MIERTA NICKI CAREN
MADELINE JEREMY ABBY PHIL TOM HEIDI SHIRLEY LEO LEEANN LO
ERIKA ALESSANDRA ADAM DANA JAN DAVID JANET ALI PETER ELI
JONAH EMMA RON CARA JULIA CHRIS STEPHANIE PAISLEY NAOMI PAU
FARLEY MICHAEL MEG GARY JOE MJ JOYCE AMY MICHELLE MEL JEI
PAM NICOLE SALLY BARB MARY BOB ARON JEREMY SANFORD MAI
JENNY JOE KATE LILY JAMES STEPHEN PEGGY MIKE SUE CINDY J
JON WENDY PATTI SCOTT DIANE DAVID JIMMY STELLA CAROLYN AN
CHERYL MICHAEL KATIE SEAN MEGAN MARK EDDIE CHERYL PILAR
JIM KATHRYN SALLY JIM DEB ANNIE ELLEN STEVE CHERYL TAHRA